MEASURING
Dedalus New Writers 1

First published in 2012 by
The Dedalus Press
13 Moyclare Road
Baldoyle
Dublin 13
Ireland

www.dedaluspress.com

Poems copyright © the respective poets
Introduction copyright © Pat Boran

ISBN 978 1 906614 58 4

All rights reserved.
No part of this publication may be reproduced in any form or by
any means without the prior permission of the publisher.

Dedalus Press titles are represented in the UK by
Central Books, 99 Wallis Road, London E9 5LN
and in North America by Syracuse University Press, Inc.,
621 Skytop Road, Suite 110, Syracuse, New York 13244.

Cover image © Tolga Sipahi / iStockphoto.com

The Dedalus Press receives financial assistance from
The Arts Council / An Chomhairle Ealaíon

MEASURING
Dedalus New Writers 1

Poems by

Marie Coveney
Clare McCotter
John Saunders

Edited by Pat Boran

DEDALUS PRESS
DUBLIN, IRELAND

ACKNOWLEDGEMENTS

Grateful acknowledgement is made to the editors of the following print and online journals in which a number of these poems have previously appeared:

Marie Coveney
Writers' Week Anthology and *Southword Journal Online;*

Clare McCotter
Blithe Spirit: Journal of the British Haiku Society, Presence, Simply Haiku, World Haiku Review, Shamrock Haiku Journal. Journal of the Irish Haiku Society, Roadrunner Haiku Journal, Haiku Scotland, Frogpond, Modern Haiku, The Haiku Foundation website, The Heron's Nest and *Contemporary Haibun Online;*

John Saunders
The Moth Magazine (Measuring), The Prairie Schooner (Kikkik), Minus Nine Squared (Jigsaw).

Contents

Introduction

MARIE COVENEY

Stone Man / 13
Keeper of the Bees / 14
Sowing / 15
Leaven / 16
Uncle / 17
The Hare's Corner / 18
Aunt Lizzy / 19
Comb-over / 20
The Pantry Door / 21
Beasts / 22
Lumumba / 23
Rhythms / 24
Our Time / 25
Field Day / 26
First-born / 27
Mother Skin / 28
Young Girl in a Green Dress / 29
Promise / 30
Seeking the Earth / 31
Cloud-soundings / 32
Coin-curse / 33

CLARE McCOTTER

A selection of haiku, tanka and haibun / 37

JOHN SAUNDERS

Convenience / 59
Days / 60
Nyaminyami / 63
Kikkik / 64
Christmas 2010 / 65
Duckling / 66
Why? / 67
Measuring / 69
Connection / 70
Lewis and Trutz / 71
Jig Saw / 72
Protection / 74
Respect / 75
The Morning the Snow Stopped / 78

Introduction

THE PRESSURES ON a small literary publishing house – perhaps particularly one that concentrates on poetry – are greater today than at any time in the recent past. Not only has the internet, and the internet book store and journal, changed the way many of us now make first contact with new poets and poetry, but the speed and appetite of the new media in general would seem to suggest that the determinedly slow-motion art form that is poetry is in some sense an anachronism in our high-velocity culture.

Such concerns are of course very much part of the day-to-day running of a small press (and at Dedalus we like to try to keep up with what's happening in the digital as well as in the physical world). Happily, though, questions of format and distribution are of less interest to poets, at least in the hot forge of poem-making: and so the essential optimism or faith in poems sustains poetry even as publishing runs around in circles, perhaps as it has always done, grappling with the implications of the latest innovation, the latest challenge.

One specific challenge for a small press such as ourselves lies in keeping up with the range of new work we receive on an ongoing basis. Twenty or so years ago, when this writer was publishing his own first poems, there were perhaps half a dozen occasional publications which catered for 'younger' poets hoping to find an outlet for a larger selection of their work than the small magazines were typically able to accommodate. In fact, almost all of the poetry presses of the time, as well as publishing new collections from individual poets, also published at least occasional 'introductory' volumes, thereby both encouraging new talent and giving that talent crucial access to a wider readership. (Few of us are like Emily Dickenson, focused and self-sufficient enough that we will not just persist but grow as writers without access to a sympathetic readership.)

Of course one of the obstacles to a publication such as the one you now hold in your hands, and one of the tacit reasons so few of even the determinedly literary presses now maintain the tradition, is the difficulty – nay, the near impossibility – of getting reviews or media coverage for such publications. If poetry is a tough station in our commercial hard times, then anthologies of up-and-coming voices might be the bleakest, most wind-swept station of all.

Even so, those of us who make time for poetry in our lives – whether as readers or writers, or both – know that good poets don't just arrive from nowhere, fully formed. Instead they grow and are nurtured by small magazines and journals and perhaps by publications such as this. If the size of its initial audience was a certain indicator of the viability of a new idea or art form, an extensive range of human pursuits (from particle physics to neurosurgery, never mind impressionism or modernism) would never have been given time to grow and evolve.

'From little things big things grow' is the folksy refrain of a favourite song by Australian singer-songwriter Paul Kelly, a narrative ballad that describes the power struggle between one rich land owner and the champion of the people who work (and suffer) under him. It's a song, of course, because Kelly is a musician and singer, and a fine one at that; but it's also a poem. And one can hear that, or see that, in the lyrics, in the way they seem able and prepared to stand apart and alone even as they also lend themselves to a singing voice. I mention the song here because its title is an endorsement of the small steps taken by a publication like this, by the creative writers who trust their words to paper and then to print, and also because it's a reminder that poems find different ways to journey in the world. Publication in book form, on the internet or radio, or as the words of songs, are not mutually exclusive categories. And neither is one form of publication superior to or more valid than any other. The purpose is to make and to keep the work available, and also to let it go, to make room for the work to come.

The poems which follow will likely in time find expression again elsewhere in the world, perhaps in full-length collections by the individual poets, perhaps on radio or other broadcast media, and no doubt at the many readings and gatherings which take place across this island and farther afield. The three poets represented here, Marie Coveney, Clare McCotter and John Saunders, work in very different forms and styles, but all have distinctive and engaging voices, voices which suggest we'll be seeing and hearing much more from them in the coming years.

– Pat Boran
March 2012

MARIE COVENEY

Marie Coveney grew up in Co. Cork and studied at the Crawford College of Art. Her poem 'Our Time' won the American-Ireland Fund Single Poem Competition at the Listowel Literary Festival in 2008. Her work has been published in: *Poetry Ireland Review, THE SHOp, The Stony Thursday Book* and *Southword Online*. She performed at the 2010 West Cork Literary Festival in 'The Next Generation Poets' reading, and The Kinsale Arts Festival 2011. She was awarded special merit in The Dromineer Literary Festival 2010 and shortlisted for the Patrick Kavanagh Award in 2010. She was published in *The Sunday Business Post*, March 2011, having featured in BBC1 TV Spotlight program.She has also been shortlisted for The Listowel Collection Competition 2011 and *The Cork Literary Review* Manuscript Competition 2011.

Stone Man

Did you see beauty in the small stream
that glistened before it sank in shale,
or the red-shanked choughs
on the grassy bank?

You nailed the slates back
when gales had spent their force.
From your hearth, smoke curled
under a peat-brown ceiling.

Stone slowly surfaced in fields
where the pink thrift shivered.
Your plough rang anvil
across the bay.

Keeper of the Bees

Father captured wild bees –
teeming brown beards that hung
from tree branches. Carried them
back to hives hidden in the orchard's
rough grass, where the tree dangled
shiny red apples, sour on the tongue.

The bees foraged and hummed in fields
clotted with clover, discordant,
when father leaned over their hives,
my brother beside him, lifting
square bullions up to the sun,
head haloed with bees – the chosen one.

Sowing

They travel to the city to order
his winter suit.

The tailor unfurls bales of pinstripe,
fleck, hound's-tooth.

With a work-reddened hand she touches
the stripe,

remembers its lines on a young man's body.

He settles on the fleck, it looks like seed
he'll set in fresh-turned drills, and in Spring –

green pinstripes.

Leaven

He came visiting when the harvest was done.
More frequent in winter – his empty house
rattling its sashes and doors.

He limped, but wanted no pity, the gleam
in his sparrow-bright eyes promised
a long night.

Our parents' first names on his lips sounded
like wild flowers: Timothy, Julia –
hinting at life before us.

His tweed coat, like a wheaten loaf rising
smelled of the rodent as he steamed
at our fire.

The stories he'd spin – Rumpelstiltskin
turning them golden. Then he'd fold himself
into his Ford and drive home.

That winter he never came calling.
The fire crackled and hissed, built magical cities
that crumbled to cinders.

We heard how he'd fallen
through worm-rotten floorboards
and lay there long nights.

Uncle

He came calling with wasp-holed windfalls
needing mother's apple strudel.

Percolated like bitter coffee, the day's gossip
became his gospel truths.

Angelic in church, Adam's apple ascending
in praise of stone saints.

At home his wife crunched yesterday's scones
brewed tealeaf prophesies.

Like Sisyphean children, we were sent to clear
rocks from his fields.

Watched him build stone enclosures, where grass
grew emerald.

His grain never lodged, machinery blades
never shattered.

While our wheat was planted too late,
potatoes had eyes like the head of Medusa.

The Hare's Corner

Gold squared in a field.
The harvester turns to face the glare.

Tines caress then grasp the trembling ears,
blades level the feet,

cutting to the blond heart, where
corncrakes streak the final strip of grain.

Leverets freeze – then rise like red rags on the blades,
young of pheasant ghost-wing the evening breeze.

The nape bristles, crew-cut-hard.

On the field's dry rim where scarlet poppies seed
a stand of wheat remains, token run for the witches' familiar.

The huge red harvest moon swells
with the blood of the sun.

Aunt Lizzy

Clad in her front and back-panelled polka-dot
pinafore, she hunts the sun's rays for dust motes.
Polishes the bell-jar that holds the snarling stoat,
wipes the iridescence on the peacock's feathers –
a thousand eyes watching from a cut-glass vase.

She skims the picture of the Navy ship
her husband sailed on. He returned from heathen England
to his sickbed, resistant to her pleading
to seek forgiveness for his sins. Priests' palaver
he called it – and died.

She has a coffin-freezer in the pantry crammed
with frost-rimed legs, a head rammed in a box
from the pig she pickled in salt peter. Broilers plucked
and ready for the pot, and the young gander
that pecked her ankle – just the once.

Comb-over

It grows thickest behind his ears, like wheat spurting
under the charged feet of a pylon.

In a foxed bathroom mirror he fashions himself
young again,

hair darkened by a slick of Brilliantine.
Arranged in a helmet to defy

the cute westerlies that swirl like cattle circling
a mart-pin.

The merciless north wind lifts the umbilical hair-ribbon,
exposing his dome, newborn.

The Pantry Door

The boys shot tin cans –
then crows from chimney tops.

Grown to men, they aimed at the sky –
pheasants fell at their feet.

Birds hung from our pantry door
tied by their long spurs,

wattles like pockets of blood,
their eyes, milk-lidded.

Flesh, the colour of saffron adorned
our table.

Tongues probed each mouthful,
tiny lead pellets tinkled on side plates –

ringing small death knells.

Beasts

You remember the smell of birth on straw,
tiny bodies nuzzling an udder that wobbled
like pink blancmange.

Cherub-faced, sated on colostrums, they dozed
under a red lamp,
their cubicle womb-like.

Now you hear squeals from the pitch-dark piggery
as they nibble each other's tails
to stubs.

One hangs halved in the mill house, severed
from snout to haunch, short hairs dusted
in meal.

Blood darkens in a tin bucket.
Saltpetre glistens in a timber tub.

Lumumba

He was a black and white sheepdog,
called after the murdered Congolese leader
whose name rumbled from our wireless.

I'd bury my nose between his dry pads –
smells of the earth
lay buried there.

He jumped through wheat fields, lodging grain,
rising pheasants. Mice and voles ran before his charge.
He was a lion in his Serengeti.

When he went missing, I lit candles, recited golden
Hail Marys. Father said he might have strayed,
others told of tinkers camping at the crossroads.

I pictured him tied to a caravan wheel, straining
to return to me. As I set out to accost them,
Mother laid a gentle hand upon my shoulder,

'Lumumba,' she said, 'was a ringleader,
he killed defenceless sheep.
Think of the lambs.'

Rhythms

A winter's evening, the barn spun with light
from a cobwebbed bulb. Rain's gentle patter
on the tin roof turns to thunder, drowning out
the machine's sucking rhythm.

Between honey-brown timbers, silent cows
chew the cud, spring green imprinted on dark pupils.
The scent of sweet hay mingles
with milk frothing.

In the crossbeams a single sparrow notes the cease of rain.
Somewhere, embedded in the rick, a broody hen sits
on her addled eggs. While the sheepdog, curled
in her golden bed nuzzles new-born pups to life.

Our Time

Outside the school window
silken dandelion seeds rose,
offering our floating thoughts,
skywards.

We sweated inside
moss-stitched jumpers,
watched chalk dust dance
in the high-window sunlight.

Encrusted in jam-jars
little gardens dribbled
with tropical rain. Peas sprouted
on damp paper.

Crackled maps hung
with blue-veined continents,
and our hands held inked estuaries,
deltas, flood-plains.

Across the pink mountains of our thumbs
red cane-welts ran. Held cradled in our laps
palms stiffened and throbbed
with pain.

Our eyes slid sideways along dried floorboards,
to where the cane sat – pointing like a gun.

The clock ticked, inched
towards three – a dandelion head quivering
with our time.
We held our breaths.

Field Day

We ran, kicking dandelion clocks,
dodging thistles and dried cowpats.
The field was decked with trestle tables
posts, pens and a large tent.

We bought Humbugs, Peggy's Legs,
shiny, gold-coin chewing gum;
took a chance on the Fortune Wheel,
then flittered pink tickets to the wind.

Willy Lynch, who gave the field free
paraded with the parish priest.
Mrs Brady's famous sponge cakes
sat on willow-pattern dinner plates.

Farmers circled, tractors smoked.
Danny just stood in mucky boots,
his brown coat belted
with hairy rope.

A swing-boat carried us high in the air.
Our stomachs lurched, wind played whirly-gigs
with our hair. A lifted plank bumped us
back to earth.

Through a gap in the hedge, we spied our school,
like a cut-out house in its concrete yard, waiting
for September – asking
to be kicked down.

First-born

My mother kept a birth caul
tucked in the side-pocket of her bag.
Forceps-like, my small fingers

would fish it out, unfold
the worn brown envelope,
hold the web-like skin up to the light.

She'd tell me once again, it was a talisman,
good-luck charm for sailors –
the look in her eyes as far away as the sea.

I didn't know it was a cherished membrane
taken from her first-born's head,
the boy who fell from his sea-blue cot.

Mother Skin

All her sisters were pale as field daisies,
but she looked good, sun-kissed and fresh
in crisp cotton dresses. Turned my father's head –
a delight to his ice-blue eyes.

She worshiped the sun, until that day –
looking for hens laying out in the bushes,
she lay down on the cool, cool grass,
closed her eyes, for just a moment.

Woke to a field undulating beneath her. Sweat
like grease on her flesh. Tethered by her skirt
she stumbled home. Lay for weeks
in a hospital bed.

Sought shade and overcast days, thereafter.
Squinted from under a wide brimmed hat.
In old age, liver spots mapped her hands,
nascent magma.

Young Girl in a Green Dress

after a painting by Henri Matisse

In a room brimming with sun and scent
you wait for him.

Dressed in a shift of the finest shot silk
shimmering with swallow motifs.

Casablanca lilies open on the sill
pistils tender and glistening,

each leaf a curled Turkish slipper.

Scent cloys the room, as twilight
creeps in.

Your dress, now a drab sack, teeming
with eyes.

The telephone squats in a corner,
mouthpiece clamped down.

Promise

Allotted a narrow strip
under rough-barked pines
we gardened in splintered sun-
light. Privet sparrows spied
as we drew finger-drills
in bone dry soil. Seed scattered
from bright packets promised:
cup and saucer Canterbury bells,
snap dragons' frilly lips, butterfly-
winged larkspur.
But the earth repelled all water
runnelling like dust-skinned snakes.
Privet thickened with the flint-
chat of sparrow. The canopy
darkened as crows crash-landed,
jostled for territory, flicking slow-
falling feathers that speared
black knives into our barren earth.
We grew covetous:
hoarded the blue of magpie,
the speckle of thrush,
heaping white stones to mark
our territory. They gleamed like bones
in a lost Eden.

Seeking the Earth

As I walk the fields I see:
the twitching antennae of hare's ears,
I see pimpernel hiding in plain sight,
I see the criminal eyes of a magpie,
I see gorse gold-gloating, blackthorn in a froth,
I see the ferreter's terrier snap its snared leg,
I see vetch, laddered leaves clambering,
a pheasant emerges, sleek as a flame,
I see the tattered scare of a crow ghost-goading
from a pole,
I see a spring trickle, peevish – it sinks again,
I see toadflax toadying, little lips aquiver
beside blue speedwell – brittle as frost,
I see the scalpel of dock, crimson-dipped,
I see the meekness of chorister-daisies,
seeking the earth – begging beheading.

Cloud-soundings

The dockside once rang with industry.
Ships clanged like giant bells, flux flaring
from their hulls.

Now small-hammer toil taps from broken-
windowed warehouses. Stacked timber
and sleek speedboats wait, ready for export.

Cranked-up cranes, their jibs disembodied
in low cloud, sing off key cries like sirens
from the deep.

The vast platform, prised by dandelions –
they grow like sun gods,
become seed-blown moons.

Coin-curse

May the ghouls of ghost estates, the gable howling
banshees, poltergeists haunt your mansion.

May your nose grow, not like Pinocchio, but the flaccid
snot-gathering snout of an elephant seal.

May love turn foul as morning breath,
your wife find redemption in a strapping milkman.

May bailiffs blitz your riches, leaving you a token slot machine
for fruit speculation.

When you speak, may your tongue become a wedged coin.

CLARE McCOTTER

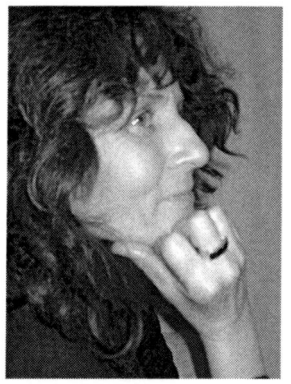

Clare McCotter has worked as a psychiatric nurse, a lecturer and an English teacher. She was awarded a Ph.D from the University of Ulster in 2005, and has published numerous peer-reviewed articles on Beatrice Grimshaw's travel writing and fiction. Her haiku, tanka and haibun have appeared in *Blithe Spirit, Presence, Haiku Scotland, Shamrock, Frogpond, The Heron's Nest, Modern Haiku, Roadrunner, Simply Haiku, World Haiku Review, Paper Wasp,* and various anthologies. Her poetry has been published in *Abridged, The SHOp, The Stinging Fly* and *Irish Feminist Review*. In 2008 she was runner-up in the Leaf Book International Poetry Competition, and winner of the IHS Dóchas Ireland Haiku Award in 2010 and 2011. She judged the British Haiku Awards 2010 and 2011. *Black Horse Running: a collection of haiku, tanka and haibun* (Alba Publishing, 2012) is her first collection. Home is Kilrea, Co. Derry.

stag with autumn cud
sapid reliquary
dark green memories

                rebel in russet
                urban fox sashaying
                down a cantaloupe moon

dusky river
swimming in pink sky
the dog otter

                liturgy of stars
                on noon's broken pavement
                a pigeon's trembling feet

stony beach
silver in a wolf moon
sheep bones

        the dead hare is gone
        among hazel roots and stars
        its imprint still warm

starlight
on leaf mulch
a worm's crystal pulse

        enfolding
        the fallen foxglove
        a slug's soft dream

evening star
a silver sapling
in the junkyard

        headstone in moonlight
        my problems
        still keeping you awake

veridical silver fish
slashing my bowl of night
meteorite

                sparkling still
                below a sky of starfish
                the ct scanner

forty seven
and no pension
all the starry heavens

                falling star
                starshaped space
                miscarriage

a pigeon's purple throat
sunstroked on the ledge below
my unturned page

for judas

as their sandals mark the hill's warm side quivering olive leaves silver the dry ebony air the only silver here not already transmuted into hanging branch and field of blood but now alone like him among judean stone and stars my flushed mouth is a flower broken centuries before in a prophet's white hand for how could I not love this man and there was night in the garden

tulips
incarnadine
his lips

        the sexton in silence
        this evening
        will come late
        for a swallow nests
        among the saints

tonight at a manger
wise men stand silent
in the amber light
from an oxen's
weeping eye

        their high country's
        dying year turns thoughts
        to her own low indigo lands
        where a man whispers
        the names of swans

the roof of her mouth
was starless ebony
at dusk an old man
speaks of the sheepdog
he worked in his youth

changing fields

for phil mccotter

it is summer and we are driving cattle through the gold dusk behind the slow swinging rumps a girl's sandals pool charcoal in the ground mist of their breath as she directs a ringle-eyed collie to the next opening in the hedge where couchant he waits while the rough rattle of hooves pass impatience or the wolf spurring him to nip the last and as they break into an awkward trot you shout from the front to take things easy – the road to new grass is long and dry a lintwhite moon already looms high when you open the gate to your six acres our best field in the girl's eyes a sea of pristine green now on this pavement where no tracks mark the dark patina of dust it is summer and we are driving cattle through the gold dusk

still night
cattle on low land –
archipelago

violet night lamplighted translucent wings

in sleep still a dancer deep iris sky

the blue beyond broken ties a wishing kite

an unforgotten hand alone in damask dark a swan

three heavy horses in rape where I can not stop

full in azure weather the condemned cow's udder

starlight moving through the scent of horses

feathering my gut with his words the rose rambles

first frost
brimming my hands
a grey mare's breath

                                        the horses are gone
                                        tonight in the far fields
                                        a single silver moth

starlight
though none are here
the scent of horses

                                        the timbre
                                        of a horse's heart
                                        winter sea

narrow lapis lake
deeper than sky
pupil of a horse's eye

horse dream

chestnut mare you carried me to this land where the cities are the colour of viridian and all our roads are water - cool opulent ovals under *apah* animate lustral lapping baptising perfectly russet hocks your forehead's crooked star sinking over my unfolded palm a salfay of serafina and siberian blue smooth on your sovereign tongue

summer dusk
a horse's soft mouth
my feeding hands

dreaming the book

the room's heart dark-seasoned under a star struck cupola refracting the hunter and his dogs - glass censer dispensing silent benediction: first snow sky's augur of forgiveness falling whiter than ever before through it I approach a desk of turkish oak where his hands offer a manuscript of sixteenth century verse all unread all miraculous in cerulean and gold

dust motes
in a lexicon of light
the library's faded colours

        red gold water
        the trout's footprints
        crossing a bedouin sun

at the burial a wasp
reminds me
of last night's dream

        may meadow at dusk
        red fox spancelled
        to a frolicking shadow

nothing surprises at the zoo
only you
grey squirrel on ash branch

        white crocus
        the pianist's trembling
        translucent hands

old medical notes
call him *imbecile*
when he thinks no one
is looking he spreads
crumbs for the starlings

        derelict house
        long vanished lawns
        only the magnolias
        do not realise
        they have gone

unopened letter
haloed in lamplight
somewhere upriver
spawn song silvering
a dark salmon night

        worse things no doubt
        than a horse being shot
        still I wonder about
        your last thought in light
        bright with rowan berries

cervine dawn

white-lichen skinned rocks shock in their geometry as windwarped trees like begging ballerinas implore some mad god of dance and everywhere the atlantic with each hard lapping clatters down a starcobbled shore while silent above it all the onyx muzzle I approach on air moving close yet never close enough until tensing in first light it flees and I bereft stoop to touch a hieroglyph of leaving touching instead a dark red heart still beating there

        cryptic love song
           her fingers in a deer's hoofprint
              at dawn

clouds in a mare's eye the fracture beyond repair

moonlight on a zinc roof dereliction music

wild geese parting the blue northern yearnings

amid all the red ink a crane fly's wing

black horse running rolling away the stone

down here in different dark hard tracks

the tattered hem of a wedding dress winter moon

here other than wind's lamentation nothing is

horse dream

capall bán carbon-heart and forest-veins your deep-draped hawthorn mane we were at the fort when hammond gave you to me finest cob ever to cut hooves on connemara rock you stood sixteen hands in a night whose amethyst soul we crossed the reins luminous with insight even when you bolted on that northern headland – leading iron splitting the ground simpatico until you rose above a field of green stars a laughing hallelujah my outstretched arms

the still earth
mingling with mine
a horse's breath

        sounding syllables
        in a name unsounded
        until tonight when the hare
        lowered her deep eyes
        in a sapphire sky

dying elsewhere
in a migrating moon
but at a derelict house
the blue hydrangea
blossoms wait

        stirring places where
        sad secrets bide
        his words are a chrysalis
        blossoming in milk
        under the frozen tides

derelict house closed
for years to storms
and strangers
the emperor's wing
enters your dark chamber

spreading in this same
place each day
his crusts and crumbs
from his park bench
the drunk gardens sky

                        the drunk recites
                  a pigeon's blue clapping
                            wings rise

      wakening
   in a scullery of stars
the wino folds her home

                    as spring hits the city
                    a drunk with a can
                    in each pocket
                    raises a jubilant hand
                    and stops the traffic

                    high open ground
                    stippled with
                    silver lark song
                    same place where
                    the body was found

lowered
on lark song
his coffin

                    amid all
                    the candles
                    a face
                    I thought
                    was hers

the fire's scent
lingering
morning moon

                    river bent barely
                    into the gold
                    unknown I
                    have come from

open door …
in the snow
angel's heart
a sparrow

horse dream

capaillín ársa was there a dream before words pendent on lemon branch like doleful white-faced mares in the ortolan's golden orchard? before lips gleamed with a brattle of broken bit with a silver insouciant *fuck it?* claretcoloured night – fingers opaline in an avalanche of mane our only rudder raddled with moonshine

rain on summer sand
a child writes
the dead pony's name

movanagher moon
> *in memory of willie mcgill*

low over movanagher wood this new year's new moon is a mercury quill inscribing diamond distances in the blue baize between of day and other as I wonder if it is a prayer or a salutation that I offer as you offered monthly until your eighty-fifth year unobstructed by any glass

off the gravel path
an old man's uplifted face
white lunar psalm

JOHN SAUNDERS

John Saunders' first collection *After the Accident* was published in 2010 by Lapwing Press, Belfast. His poems have appeared in *Revival, The Moth Magazine, Crannog, Prairie Schooner Literary Journal* (Nebraska), *Sharp Review, The Stony Thursday Book, Boyne Berries, Riposte* and online in *The Smoking Poet, Minus Nine Squared, The First Cut* and *The Weary Blues*. John is the Director of Shine, a national voluntary mental health organisation. He lives in Co. Offaly.

Convenience

Tonight after dinner I will wash and dry
the single plate and fork, throw away
perishable food, turn off the heating,
set the phone to answer itself, check
the lights and doors (remembering
to leave one unlocked) and retire
to my bedroom. I will undress, order
my clothes neatly in the wardrobe,
place the washing in the waste basket.
I will carefully stack my loose change
on the dressing table in the company
of my wallet, car keys, mobile phone
(turned to silent), my address book.
I will use the toilet, brush my teeth,
have a shower. Naked and clean
I will slip between the white cotton sheets
and centre myself. I will lie supine,
the duvet over my face, inviting
sleep to take me.
While waiting, I will review the journey
of my life, the high points of acclamation,
failures of achievement, accidents
of misfortune. I will consider my entourage
of friends and thank them, exonerate
those fallen away, ask forgiveness
of people hurt. I will think of my children,
wish them the goodness of life,
hand into their care this earth, the planets
and stars. I will turn off the bedside lamp.
I will not set the alarm.

Days

Monday

"After Do Nothing Day" arrives without ceremony,
taking over as the first, blue day, washing day,
after the chores time to look beyond the now
over the clothesline, at the yellow Moon,
that dry dusty world. All that is left,
the solid flag and footprints, the scrap yard of Apollo,
ice cold metal reflecting the blue of this globe.

Tuesday

The second day, Viternik in Russian,
first of the Nordic Gods or, perhaps
Anglo Saxon, Tiu. A soft sound, labia shaped
to a kiss. Mars shines bright red tonight
as they slip underground, become
invisible. Lovers always win, losers
can sometimes love.

Wednesday

Odin, Chief of the Pantheon, mercurial,
caught in the middle of this time
looking for Freyja, she hiding in the future,
nothing to do but wait, silent and invisible
for the ravens to return with their wisdom.
Watch the temperature change today,
the children full of woe.

Thursday

Thunder rolls over the day, the pressure
is low, Cumulonimbus gathering force,
rainfall. Shopping day, hunting
and gathering, Jupiter lines up with mars,
sixpence for a comic, a story to be told,
a lesson learned. Let not war destroy
the crops and the people.

Friday

The King of days is here. Odin is happy,
Freyja has turned up. A day of rest for some,
others winding down, holy day in the east,
fish fast day in the West. Let us prepare
for the end. Venus Shines. Love is about.
What of memory? A shadow on the lung
of time, benign or malignant, always dark.

Saturday

This is the Sabbath for some, a celebration
of the harvest. Dies Saturni, when crime
is not punished, servants waited upon,
revelry enjoyed. Saturn will party tonight.
The tribes gather to go to war,
bring home the spoils, celebrate victory.
Sweet babies sleep in cotton nests.

Sunday

The first day of the week, usurped
by Monday, Sunnendaeg, day of God's
rest and resurrection. Brightest and hottest
star in our galaxy, life giver, warming the soil.
The furthest from us and the most needed,
A distant friend, worthy of worship, Sun god
heed my prayers.

Nyaminyami

It is surprising that I keep on my office
windowsill a representation of a god.
In the late fifties they dammed
the Zambezi, flooded the valley
and created Lake Kariba.
Nyaminyami, a water god
of the Batonka tribe lives there.

Half serpent, half fish
carved from wood he sits close
as if to protect and perhaps
to prompt me to believe
beyond reason that somewhere
above or below water a benevolent
being is shielding me from harm.

Kikkik

The caribou did not appear that terrible spring
leaving the death white winter to starve the tribe,
the old, crippled and sick giving up their used lives,
the ties of the living splintering like ice;
the power of hunger.

They fought over scarcity as when her half brother
pushed by the rage of starvation shot her husband.
She buried his freezing body, bade her child
fetch the sharpest knife, stalked him under dark
and sliced wide open his hollow stomach;
the power of love.

Against the swirling blades of snow and sleet,
her five children wasting, they trekked
across the endless empty white
until dragged under the drifts.
She wrapped the youngest two in seal skins;
the power of instinct.

They found them before the wolves –
coffined in the skins.

Christmas 2010

And hollow peace bursts
over the land, another birth
to celebrate, prayers for some
who do not need them

while dark birds gather,
a flock of truth beginning
its exit from hopelessness,
their cold wings prepared.

A journey to death
or glory, the tinsel
fading from the start.
Who knows how it ends?

We can sing to the empty
sky, our pockets cold,
the long hand of the night
fisted dark and deep.

Hold the vision there,
mark out the ground,
dig for your sorrows,
let them be found.

Duckling

His head hangs in shame
as if hiding from my gaze.
On barren days I talk to him.
He has never replied,
instead he lies on the soft
nest of my desk, an orphan
of the anatidae family.
It is wrong to say he is ugly,
more, scrawny in an embryonic way
with his soft egg yolk feathers,
his black pin-head eyes
and his untried natal beak.
He is a fragile creature
like the wispy girl
with shell-like skin who
on her departure said
when you look at him
you will think of me.

Why?

It's not that she wasn't pretty
and without natural ability,
that her conversations weren't pithy,
her jokes in company not witty,
that she could sing off key, a ditty
from the back catalogue of Conway Twitty,
that her thinning hair looked bitty
so that she became an object of pity.
Nor was it to do with the gritty
way she hugged me like a smithy
especially when she was tipsy
like that evening on the settee,
I reading the story of Walter Mitty,
she watching *Sex in the City*
when I sensed an atmosphere of enmity
from which there is no indemnity
leaving me in the proximity
of unpredictable acts of hostility
resulting in my indignity
as she bounced about with alacrity
while I prayed to the Holy Trinity
to rescue me from the vicinity
and hide me under a cloak of anonymity.
No – it was not the threat to my credibility,
the loss of personal integrity
or the gazes of incredulity
she fired at me with regularity,
the way she spoke with audacity
as if I lacked capacity,
her lack of veracity,
the poverty of her generosity,

the sling of her high velocity
tongue, irritation at her verbosity.
Not even the ferocious atrocity
that resulted from her mendacity
or the blinding luminosity
of her blatant dishonesty.
No – we simply fell out of love.

Measuring

In the shade of a November evening
we could be found in the twelve by eight
breeze block back yard shed lit by a bare
forty watt tungsten, inches deep in the slush
of sawdust and shavings, measuring
and marking and measuring again
the lengths of four by two or three by six
before gently pressing them against
the softly humming saw, each piece
shaping to its future.
Few words were spoken but in the hush
you could cut the air of satisfaction
with a blade, when the two ends joined flush.

Connection

In the constant chase of its own ferromagnetic tail
Your Geomag spinning top gives the hump
to the brake factor of friction, the apathy
of waning momentum, creates the illusion
of persistent revolution in space not unlike
the planets in ponderous orbit on the axes
of their own insouciance in the vast and limitless
explosion of universe, the prevailing domain
of our poor existence where despite the laws
of attraction our earthly trysts are marked
as equal and opposite forces, unable to locate,
polar opposites, repelled, each of us wishing
for the stuck-together-ness of magnetic attraction
where we share the ions of human connection.

Lewis and Trutz

Collision theory and angles of interest, the dynamics of change,
principles of statistical mechanics, the energetics of science
tell you how fast or slow the products of chemistry may form
in a chemical reaction, given that all such reactions are
a result of collisions between atoms, molecules and ions.

During World War One, itself a collision of imperialist nations
while men wearing bell shaped metal helmets splatter
and bloody it out on the fields of France and Belgium, two equal
and opposite chemists autonomously and simultaneously work
it out in the battlefields of their British and German laboratories.

Some collisions occur at right energies and angles to break
old bonds, release heat. The energy of reactant molecules
against the number possessing that amount of energy
is the Maxwell-Boltzmann distribution which is Gaussian,
that is to say bell shaped like those hats in the trenches.

The rate of reaction is directly proportional to the temperature
and concentration which explains why on the field of battle
when the forces strike each other, things get very hot.

Jig Saw

i

Luther pressed the blade to skin,
shaved until smooth, looked again
at his face, knew it was too late,
the canal dredged as he splashed.
He dressed casually taking care to match,
threw the key under the mat.
If he remained he would miss the train.

ii

Mai stopped to listen, heard the click,
wondered if he would come back,
picked up the other shoe, prepared
to leave. *Dinner at The Locke
would be good, a chance to reminisce.
How would she manage the grass verge
in those high heels?*

iii

Slone sat at his worn out desk,
re sorted the photographs.
Passion is the girlfriend of crime
and the relationship is just fine.
When he found the key he counted
the parts that added up to the whole.
Now he needed to know her name.

iv

Local drove the car to the water,
hand braked, left it idling.
The carbon monoxide got him
just before the engine cut.
They found the body cold,
no papers to say who to tell.
The canal frozen, unsearchable.

v

Carla fingered the cut edges.
A serrated blade but what type?
She looked at the distressed face.
It's not possible to die without
pain, the price of passage.
She closed the file. Still no motive,
weapon. Not much to go on.

Protection

Always protect the wood he said,
me at his side holding the brush
painting the sides of the bed.
Always protect the wood he said
I not sure what was in his head
until he raised his hand to touch.
Always protect the wood he said
me at his side holding the brush.

Respect

Father Byrne, Father Browne
walk the walled gardens, soutanes
gathered off the wet ground,
greasy hands on black cloth
missals clasped close to chest
sorrowful mysteries, sacred hearts blessed.

Here is the soft focus across the yard.
He sees every face from the dark of his mind,
number one, number two, stand up,
wipe that grin boy, you whingeing pup,
stop that crying boy.

Remember to show him respect,
genuflect, kiss his ring.
He will touch your cheek –
expect him to touch your cheek.

In the cool of the afternoon
empty exhausted classrooms,
chalk dust on desks,
ink stains on shirts and dresses,
a time for play, study time,
catch up time – *stand up,*
sit down, give me your hand.

There now, gentle – don't cry,
Remember – quiet, don't cry, don't.
He sees all things, he is everywhere,
on the street, in your house, in your room,
in your heart. Fingers to your lips –
ciúnas.

After Mass – take off the Chasuble,
Cincture, Amice, Alb.
Come here, hold this and this.
What's your name? Ah yes.
I knew your older brother.
A fine boy, are you another?

In the unlit Chancel, head lowered
at a side alter – uncontrollable.
All silent – words not allowed,
words not able to describe –

the sorrowful tears,
the agony in the garden,
the spit in the face,
the slap on the cheek
the pull of the hair,
the scourge of the skin,
the crown of thorns,
the pierce of the spear,
the stigmata,
the stigmata,
forever and ever …

Father Byrne, Father Browne in the parlour,
breakfast after Mass, chatter of the day,
sports, baptism, confessions, altar boy's tea.
Remember to genuflect, kiss his ring,
show him respect.

Do you reject Satan? – I do
Do you believe in Jesus Christ? – I do.
Do you believe in the most Holy Trinity? – I do.

*I confirm you – touch you in Christ,
a soldier of Christ, body of Christ,
your body of Christ.*

Here is the hard focus, here is the view.
all twisted and turned, inside out, outside in.
Here is the boy, here is the man.
Remember, show him respect.

The Morning the Snow Stopped

It was the silence that shocked,
the city muted by the quiet
of snow and I remembered a time
when silence was a rule of survival,
to speak was to be punished,
the consequence of expression.

When it happened, I was numbed
not by the swell of warm blood,
not even by the hole in my heart
but by his embrace of regret
and his breath on my scalded face
as icy as the morning the snow stopped.

Lightning Source UK Ltd.
Milton Keynes UK
UKOW052111250412

191447UK00001B/3/P

9 781906 614584